P9-DNO-804

Moments for Friends

by Robert Strand

First printing, December 1995
Sixth printing, January 2006

Copyright © 1995 by New Leaf Press. All rights reserved. No part of this book may be used or reproduced in any manner whatsoever without written permission of the publisher except in the case of brief quotations in articles and reviews. For information write: New Leaf Press, Inc., P.O. Box 726, Green Forest, AR 72638.

ISBN: 0-89221-301-9
Library of Congress Catalog Number: 95-69897

Cover design by Left Coast Design, Portland, OR.

All Scripture references are from the New International Version, unless otherwise noted.

New Leaf Press
A Division of New Leaf Publishing Group
www.newleafpress.net

Printed in China

Presented to:

_____

Presented by:

_____

Date:

_____

Day 1
My Best Friend

The late Dr. W.L. Stidger, while pastoring a church following World War II, asked a young man from his congregation, a returning naval officer this question: "What was your most exciting adventure during the war?" And here is the reply:

We were cruising through a submarine zone in the North Atlantic and knew that a wolf pack of enemy subs was near. Naturally we were all alert to the danger. It was early morning and not my watch, but I was up much before dawn on that fateful morning. I felt that I just wanted to be on the bridge, because I was also afraid. We were a troopship carrying 10,000 soldiers on their way to Europe. I had a great sense of responsibility for those American G.I.'s and their safety.

About half an hour after I went up on the bridge with the captain, the sun just barely began to come up out of the east horizon. We watched in fascination. It was beautiful. As we were looking at it through our glasses, we both spotted it at the same time! We watched the white wake of a torpedo headed straight for our ship! It was a terrorizing thing! We couldn't dodge it . . . we had no time to maneuver our cumbersome ship out of its path. The captain turned to me, thinking of those 10,000 boys asleep down in the holds and said, "This is it."

My heart stood still. Of course, the captain called all hands to their battle stations, but it seemed like such a futile gesture.

Then . . . suddenly, something happened which none of us had even considered. There was a destroyer riding to our port, battling the waves. The skipper of that smaller ship had seen the same thing that we had seen from our bridge . . . the enemy torpedo out of that Nazi wolf pack of subs headed straight for the middle of our ship.

That young skipper instructed his engine room: "All engines ahead flank!" This headed his destroyer straight into the path of that torpedo. It struck full impact about midship and sank in less than 10 minutes with most of her crew going down with her, including that young skipper. He knew when he gave that order that he and his crew would be lost . . . but he didn't hesitate a single second. He willingly gave himself for more than 10,000 others.

That young skipper? He was my best friend!

Today's Quote: *Actions, not words, are the proof positive of love.*

Today's Verse: Greater love has no one than this, that he lay down his life for his friends (John 15:13).

Day 2
Brotherhood

This story was told by Bob Tuttle, professor at Fuller Theological Seminary, and is alleged to be a true story that happened to the son of the Rev. Reuben Job, a United Methodist minister:

The boy (let's call him Billy) was attending his first day at junior high school. It began with an assembly, one feature of which was the introduction of all the homeroom teachers.

First to be introduced was Miss Smith, and the ninth graders, knowing Miss Smith to be an easy grader and not much of a disciplinarian, all began to cheer: "Yea, Miss Smith! Right on, Miss Smith!"

The next to be introduced was Mr. Brown, who was a young and popular teacher, a special favorite. This time the eighth graders joined in the thundering approval: "Yea, Mr. Brown! Hurrah for Mr. Brown!"

By the time the next teacher was introduced, even the ignorant seventh graders were getting into the spirit of the thing. Then they introduced Mr. Johnson, an older teacher who was reputed to be the hardest grader and least sympathetic teacher in the school as well as a strong disciplinarian. The cat calls began: "Booo, Mr. Johnson! Hiss . . . Mr. Johnson!"

The pain was evident on old Mr. Johnson's face. Suddenly Billy stood up in the middle of the bleachers and shouted, "Shut up! He's my father!" The noise died as they clearly got the message . . . *"Cool it, Johnson's son is here."*

That afternoon when school was out, Billy raced home. His father met him, "Son, what's wrong?"

"Dad, I've got to talk to you. I told a lie in school today."

So Billy told the story. When he was through, his dad put his arm around him and said, "It's all right, son. You didn't really tell a lie . . . you just got the family members mixed up. Mr. Johnson's not your father; he's your brother."

Brotherhood . . . have you given much thought to this concept lately? There is a common bond because we are all human beings . . . but beyond that? Do we really care enough to stand up and be counted on when it comes to helping a friend, a neighbor, a sister, or a brother?

Today's Quote: *You can't spell "brothers" and not spell "others."* — Baptist Standard

Today's Verse: Keep on loving each other as brothers. Do not forget to entertain strangers, for by so doing some people have entertained angels without knowing it (Heb. 13:1–2).

Day 3
Friends Understand

Bob Weber, former president of Kiwanis International, tells the following story. He had been the special guest speaker to a Kiwanis club in a small town and was spending the night with a club member who was a farmer, on the outskirts of the town. He and the farmer had just gotten comfortable on the front porch when a newsboy delivered the evening paper. The boy noticed the sign: PUPPIES FOR SALE! He got off his bike and asked, "How much do you want for the pups, mister?"

"Twenty-five dollars each, son."

Bob Weber said the boy's face dropped. "Well, sir, could I at least see them anyway?"

The farmer whistled and in a moment the mother dog came bounding around the corner of the house followed by four of the cutest puppies you would ever see, wagging their tails and yipping happily. Finally, another pup, a straggler, came around the house, dragging one hind leg. "What's the matter with that puppy, mister?" the boy asked.

"Well, son, that puppy is crippled. We had the vet x-ray her. There's no hip joint and that leg will never be right."

To the amazement of both men, the boy dropped the bike, reached for his collection bag and took out two quarters. "Please, mister," the boy pleaded, "I want to buy that pup. I'll pay you 50 cents every week until the 25 dollars is paid. Honest I will, mister."

The farmer replied, "But, son, you don't seem to understand. That pup will never be able to run or jump. She is going to be a crippled dog forever. Why in the world would you want such a useless pup as that? I'll be glad to give her to you, she's not worth anything, anyway."

The boy paused for a moment, then reached down to pull up his pant's leg, exposing a leg brace. The boy answered, "Mister, that pup is going to need someone who understands her to help her in life!"

And . . . don't we all?! I don't know of a person in this world who doesn't need friends and someone to understand and to care and to love! Do you? We all need to build our life on relationships and good times with good friends.

The greatest Friend in this world is the friend above all others. A friend who willingly laid down His life for you and me. He set the pattern for human friends and relationships. His name is Jesus Christ, known as the "friend of sinners."

Today's Quote: *The very best recipe for making friends is to be one yourself.*

Today's Verse: A man of many companions may come to ruin, but there is a friend who sticks closer than a brother (Prov. 18:24).

Day 4
The Power of Friendship

As a part of an assignment for a doctoral thesis, a college student spent a year with a group of Navajo Indians on a reservation in the Southwest. As she did her research she lived with one family, sleeping in their hut, eating their food, working with them, and generally living the life of a twentieth-century Navajo Indian.

The old grandmother of the family spoke no English at all, yet a very close bond formed between these two. In spite of the language difference, they shared the common language of love and understood each other. Over the months the student learned a few phrases of Navajo, and the grandmother picked up a little of the English language.

When it was time for the student to return to the campus, the tribe held a going-away celebration. It was marked by sadness since the young woman had become close to the whole village and all would miss her.

As she prepared to get up into the pickup truck and leave, the old grandmother came to tell her goodbye, personally. With tears streaming from her eyes, she placed her gnarled, weathered hands on either side of the young woman's face, looked directly into her eyes, and said in her broken, halting English, "I like me best when I'm with you."

And isn't that just the way we feel when we are in the presence of good friends? Friends see us as worthy and valuable when we spend time together. Friends help overlook the hurts, the cares, the disappointments of our lives. Friends are spirit-lifters. Friends help each other's self-esteem. Friends place great value on each other.

Edwin Markham, poet, was asked which of his poems he valued the most. He replied, "How can you choose between your own children?" He then went on to voice his opinion that his four lines called "Outwitted" might have the best-lasting qualities because love lasts:

> He drew a circle that shut me out.
> Heretic, rebel, a thing to flout.
> But Love and I had the wit to win:
> We drew a circle that took him in!

To be conformed to the image of Jesus Christ, the greatest of all friends, is to hopefully generate in others the old Indian grandmother's response: "I like me best when I'm with you."

Today's Quote: *You can make more friends in two months by becoming interested in other people than you can in two years by trying to get people interested in you.* — Dale Carnegie

Today's Verse: And the scripture was fulfilled that says, "Abraham believed God, and it was credited to him as righteousness," and he was called God's friend (James 2:23).

Day 5
To Be a Friend . . . Start with Yourself

The following was inscribed on the tomb of an Anglican bishop (A.D. 1100) among the crypts of Westminster Abbey located in London:

When I was young and free and my imagination had no
 limits,
I dreamed of changing the world.
As I grew older and wiser, I discovered the world would
 not change,
 so I shortened my sights somewhat and
 decided to change only my country.
But it, too, seemed immovable.

As I grew into my twilight years,
 in one last desperate attempt,
 I settled for changing only my family,
 those closest to me, but alas,
 they would have none of it.
And now as I lie on my deathbed, I suddenly realize:
If I had only changed myself first,
 then by example I would have changed my family.

> From their inspiration and encouragement,
> I would have been able to better my country and,
> who knows, I may have even changed the world.
> (Anonymous)

Here's the secret to change anything in life . . . be it life, friendships, relationships, concepts, life principles, or work. It all begins with ME, myself, and I!

Today's Quote: *Wise is the person who fortifies their life with friendships.*

Today's Verse: Therefore, everyone who hears these words of mine and puts them into practice is like a wise man who built his house on the rock (Matt. 7:24).

Old friends, old scenes
will lovelier be
As more of heaven
in each we see.

John Keble (1792–1866)

Day 6
Costly Friendship

This story comes out of World War II and details one particular bombing run over the German city of Kassel. Here's the story as told by Elmer Bendiner:

> Our B-17 (the Tondelayo) was barraged by flack from Nazi anti-aircraft guns. That was not unusual, but on this particular occasion our gas tanks were hit. Later, as I reflected on the miracle of a 20 millimeter shell piercing the fuel tank without touching off an explosion, our pilot, Bohn Fawkes, told me it was not quite that simple.

> On the morning following the raid, Bohn had gone down to ask our crew chief for that shell as a souvenir of unbelievable luck. The crew chief told Bohn that not just one shell but 11 had been found in the gas tanks . . . 11 unexploded shells where only one was sufficient to blast us out of the sky. It was as if the sea had been parted for us. Even after 35 years, so awesome an event leaves me shaken, especially after I heard the rest of the story from Bohn.

> He was told that the shells had been sent to the armorers to be defused. The armorers told him that Intelligence had picked them up. They could not say why at the time, but Bohn eventually sought out the answer.

Apparently when the armorers opened each of those shells, they found no explosive charge. They were as clean as a whistle and just as harmless. Empty? Not all of them! One contained a carefully rolled piece of paper. On it was a scrawl in Czech. The Intelligence people scoured our base for a man who could read Czech. Eventually, they found one to decipher the note. It set us marveling. Translated, the note read: "This is all we can do for you now."*

A story like that can give you goose bumps! Incredible! Little acts can amount to something as large as saving another's life. I wonder if the unknown Czech munitions worker ever got found out? Were more involved in this act of bravery? What a fantastic contribution nameless people can accomplish when they persevere in small acts of kindness. Another lesson learned in building friendships that last and are meaningful . . . if you put nothing into it, don't expect to get something back.

*Elmer Bendiner, *The Fall of Fortresses*.

Today's Quote: *Often, true friendship is just another way to spell perseverance.*

Today's Verse: All the saints send you greetings, especially those who belong to Caesar's household (Phil. 4:22).

Day 7
The Human Presence

Dr. Paul Brand, in his book *Fearfully and Wonderfully Made,* tells this story:

> As an intern on night duty in a London hospital, I called on 81-year-old Mrs. Twigg. This spry, courageous lady had been battling cancer of the throat . . . but even with a raspy hoarse voice she remained witty and happy. Surgeons had removed her larynx and malignant tissue around it.
>
> She seemed to be making a good recovery until 2:00 a.m. one morning, when I was urgently summoned. She was sitting on the bed, leaning forward, blood spilling from her mouth. Immediately I guessed that an artery had eroded. I knew no way to stop the bleeding other than to thrust my finger into her mouth and press on the pulsing spot. I explored with my finger until I found the artery and pressed it shut.
>
> Nurses cleaned up around her face while Mrs. Twigg recovered her breath. Fear slowly drained from her as she began to trust. After 10 minutes had passed and she was breathing normally again, with her head tilted back, I tried to remove my finger to replace it with an instrument. Each time I removed my finger, blood spurted afresh and Mrs. Twigg panicked. Her jaw

trembled, her eyes bulged, and she forcefully gripped my arm. We settled into position. My right arm crooked behind her head, supporting her. I could see in her intense blue eyes a resolution to maintain that position for days if necessary, I could sense her mortal fear. She knew, as I did, if we relaxed our awkward posture, she would bleed to death. We sat like that for nearly two hours. I, an intern in my twenties, and this 81-year-old woman clung to each other because we had no other choice.

The surgeon came and Mrs. Twigg and I, still entwined together in this strange embrace, were wheeled into the operating room. With everyone poised, I eased my finger out of her mouth . . . the blood clot held . . . her hand continued to clutch my shoulder and her eyes stayed on my face. In those two hours we had become almost one person.*

When pain or need or emergency strikes . . . it's the PRESENCE of another human being that really counts!

*Paul Brand and Philip Yancey, *Fearfully and Wonderfully Made* (Grand Rapids, MI: Zondervan, 1980), page 201–203, condensed, adapted.

Today's Quote: *It seems that a friend in need is about the only kind a person has these days.*

Today's Verse: A despairing man should have the devotion of his friends (Job 6:14).

Day 8
Everybody Should Have a Friend Like . . .

Just about everybody knows the Jim Brady story . . . how the big, bluff, quick-witted "Bear," only two months after becoming White House press secretary, was shot in the head during the attempted assassination of President Reagan and how he has fought his way back from brain surgery and the enduring damage from the stray bullet.

Not many people know, however, about the ceaseless single-minded devotion of Bob Dahlgren, a man who loved Brady like himself.

A few months ago, Bob Dahlgren died in his sleep, at 52 years of age. It didn't even make the morning news. But during the long months following the shooting, it was Dahlgren who took the vigil with Brady's wife, Sarah, through the long series of brain operations. It was Dahlgren and his wife Suzie who took the Bradys' young son Scott into their home through the early days of the ordeal.

It was Dahlgren who helped recovery by arranging convivial "happy hours" with Brady's friends by his hospital bedside.

As Brady recovered and was able, in a wheelchair, to return to a semi-normal life, it was Dahlgren, always Dahlgren, who scouted out the advance arrangements, who helped load and unload his friend from the specially equipped van in which Brady did most of his traveling.

It was Dahlgren who helped Sarah field the interminable questions about Brady's health and who spent countless hours keeping Brady's friends posted on his condition, who dealt with the doctors, lawyers, exploiters, bandwagon-climbers. It was Dahlgren who helped organize a foundation to assure financial support for the family.

For more than four and one-half years after Brady was shot, Bob Dahlgren devoted virtually all his time to the man he loved. And he did so with little recognition, and no hint of seeing anything in return. Never, ever did Dahlgren complain or hesitate when needed. As Dr. Arthur Kobrine, the surgeon who lived through Brady's long ordeal with him, once said, "Everyone should have a friend like Bob Dahlgren!"*

It has been said, "It's the thought that counts." Do you know what? It's not really the thought that counts. What really counts in friendship is action! We need more than words to make friendships happen and last!

*Raymond Coffey, *Pasadena Star News*, November 3, 1985.

Today's Quote: *Today, more than ever, there is an increased need to be in touch with people. We must learn to balance the material wonders of technology with the spiritual demands of our human nature.* — John Naisbitt

Today's Verse: Dear children, let us not love with words or tongue but with actions and in truth (1 John 3:18).

Day 9
Inclusive Love

It happened in World War II as our GIs were making their dash from the south, Italy and the Mediterranean, towards Germany. As part of this campaign, there were little side battles fought along the way. There were pockets of resistance that didn't require the entire army that Patton was leading . . . but some small platoons were dispatched to quell or recapture or liberate many towns.

One of these small squads was off into the hills of France and a small skirmish took place. Our GI's were pinned down by enemy fire, enough to hold them for an hour or two. There was only one casualty. He was a favorite among the other guys . . . but he also had two very special friends. The three of them had been inseparable and had become bosom buddies.

There was a problem. They were separated from their main unit by quite a few miles and really had no way to carry the body out. They desperately wanted to give him a dignified burial, and after talking with their sergeant it was decided to do it, if possible, in the nearby village. The two friends made their way to the village and found a cemetery. It was a Roman Catholic cemetery — the only one in the village. There was a possible problem. The dead GI was a Protestant.

When the two friends managed to find the priest in charge of the cemetery they requested permission to bury their friend. The priest refused because the dead soldier was not a Catholic. When the priest saw their disappointment as they turned to leave, he called out to them to stay. He then explained that they could bury their friend outside the fence, but next to the cemetery. A simple service was held, a few words were said, and they left immediately to return to their platoon.

Later, when they had some leave coming, the two friends returned to the village and the cemetery to visit their friend's grave. They couldn't find it. Their search led them back to the same priest and, of course, they asked him what had happened to the grave of their fallen friend. The priest told them that during the night following the burial, he had been unable to sleep because he had made them bury their friend outside the fence. So, in the middle of the night, he got up and moved the fence to include their dead soldier friend.

In Jesus Christ, God has moved the fence to include all, even the undeserving. Can we follow this example and move the fence, too?

Today's Quote: *We make a living by what we get out of life but we make a life by what we give.*

Today's Verse: For John the Baptist came neither eating bread nor drinking wine, and you say, "He has a demon." The son of Man came eating and drinking, and you say, "Here is a glutton and a drunkard, a friend of tax collectors and sinners" (Luke 7:33–34).

Day 10
Killing the Rat

Some years ago, during the pioneer days of aviation, when things were new and flight was in its infancy, things were pretty crude. The sophistication and technology of our day was unheard of. There were problems and dangers which present no problem to us today. With that background in mind this story makes sense.

A brave pilot was making a flight around the world in one of those earlier, crudely built airplanes. It was built with a wooden frame and fabric covered the frame. Very fragile. On this particular leg of his journey, he had been in the air about two hours since his last landing, when he heard a noise in the plane. He looked all around, curious, then was alarmed when he recognized it as the gnawing of a rat! He realized that while his plane had been on the ground a rat had gotten in the plane, somehow. The danger of the rat was that it could easily gnaw through a vital cable or control line or even one of the important wooden struts. It was a very serious problem.

What to do? He was anxious and concerned. He was about two hours from his next landing strip. Perhaps we can appreciate his dilemma. He tried to think of a solution as he flew . . . then it dawned on him — the rat was a rodent. It was not made for heights, it was made for the ground and under the ground living. That presented the solution . . . therefore the pilot began to climb until he was flying at an altitude of more than 20,000 feet. Soon the gnawing ceased. The rat was dead! The rat couldn't survive in the atmosphere at that height. More than two hours later the pilot brought the plane safely to the next landing field and looked through the plane until he found the dead rat!

I can think of many kinds of rats that can kill a friendship . . . worry, fear, dishonesty, gossip, anger, and lying, to name a few, and you perhaps have more to add to this list. How do we rid ourselves of such rats which can gnaw and destroy relationships? The solution is really quite simple. Such things cannot live or breathe in the atmosphere of the secret places of the Most High. Such things die when we ascend to the Lord through prayer, reading His Word, and a commitment to follow Him. Here is one of the major keys to being a friend and making friends. The things which seek to destroy your friendships can be put aside into perspective in the presence of the Most High God.

Today's Quote: *Worry is a thin stream of fear trickling through the mind. If encouraged, it cuts a channel into which all other thoughts are drained.* — Arthur Somers Roche

Today's Verse: We ought always to thank God for you, brothers, and rightly so, because your faith is growing more and more, and the love every one of you has for each other is increasing (2 Thess. 1:3).

Day 11
The Greatest Friend of All

Arthur Ray Ebersol had drowned! It happened on one of those beautiful beaches in southern California. Someone had called 911 and now the paramedics were frantically working over his lifeless body. The frantic father was begging the paramedics and his son to start his breathing again.

The pastor, the Rev. Jess Moody, had also been called along with the medical emergency number. When he arrived he took in this entire scene as he approached the tight circle of people around the drowned young man. He moved through the crowd and put an arm around Arthur's dad. The only sounds were the pleadings of the father and the sounds of the equipment and the whispered commands between the working paramedics. Then . . . somewhere in the background, Pastor Moody became aware of a voice — female, soprano . . . clear as crystal, a voice ringing with hope!

All eyes turned in the direction of the song. It was Arthur's mother sitting in the cab of the paramedic's ambulance. She was looking up through the sun-roof and affirming her faith skyward in song:

> I've seen the lightning flashing, I've heard the thunder roll,
> I've felt sin's breakers dashing, trying to conquer my soul.
> I've heard the voice of Jesus telling me still to fight on.
> He promised never to leave me, never to leave me alone.

No! Never alone. No! Never alone.
He promised never to leave me,
Never to leave me alone! (Anonymous song writer)

The greatest friend in all the world? Jesus Christ the Son of the living God has promised that even in the most difficult of life's circumstances . . . He is there! His promise is sure! The guarantees of His presence are promised to all who are part of the family of God. So the bottom line question to you is: Have you invited Him to be your Lord and Saviour? This is the point at which this relationship begins.

Today's Quote: *You need Jesus, Jesus needs you, and the world needs both.*

Today's Verse: God has said, "Never will I leave you; never will I forsake you." So we say with confidence, "The Lord is my helper; I will not be afraid. What can man do to me?" (Heb. 13:5–6).

*A friend is a person
with whom I may think aloud.*

Ralph Waldo Emerson (1803–1882)

Day 12
Relative Importance

George had a friend with a very inflated opinion of himself. As a friend should, George decided to help his friend lose this quirk. Subtly, George mentioned that he knew Jay Leno. The friend said, "Oh yeah — prove it!" So in a few minutes of driving they were in front of this huge house overlooking the beach at Malibu. It was most impressive with the gates and yard and imposing structure. After knocking, out came Jay who immediately said, "Come on in, George, and bring your friend!"

On the way home, this friend grudgingly said, "Okay, so you know Jay Leno."

Obviously this was not enough, so George let it slip, offhandedly, "Yes, Jay and I and the president are quite well acquainted."

The friend tossed his head and shouted, "Now, that's too much. . . . I'll pay the airfare . . . let's go to DC and we'll see about that!"

At the White House, they had just arrived and out came President Clinton to greet them saying, "Hi George. Come on in, George, old buddy, and bring your friend."

Later, George's friend looked around sheepishly and admitted, "Well, yeah, you do know the president."

George sensed his friend needed further deflation, so he casually remarked, "Yes, but you know the pope has an even nicer office than the president has."

"What?!" yelled his wide-eyed friend. "You know the pope? I'll put up $10,000 that you can't even get in to see the pope!"

In a few days they were in Rome, with George knocking on a door to the Vatican. A cardinal came out, extending his hand to George, saying, "Your friend will have to stay outside, but come on in, George, what a delight to have you again."

About an hour went by, when out came the pope onto the balcony, waving to the crowd, and with one arm around George, he made his speech to the gathered crowd in St. Peter's Square.

Later, outside, George looked around for his friend and found him out cold in the courtyard. George rushed over and helped his friend up and apologized for shocking him so much. But his friend simply shook his head and mumbled, "It's not that you knew the pope. It was the crowd! They kept asking each other, 'Who's that guy with George?' "

Today's Quote: *When a person has climbed high on the ladder of success, too often, some friends will begin to shake the ladder.*

Today's Verse: Do not exalt yourself in the king's presence, and do not claim a place among great men; it is better for him to say to you, "Come up here," than for him to humiliate you before a nobleman (Prov. 25:6–7).

The High Cost of Caring

At the 1980 International Youth Triennium in Bloomington, Indiana, Professor Bruce Riggins of McCormick Theological Seminary was speaking before 3,800 young attendees. In his message he shared the story of a lady who had impressed him in an amazing way with her dedicated Christian ministry to the underprivileged people in London, England. He was so taken with her lifestyle and ministry that he asked her what had inspired her Christian faith and the actions of her life.

She told him that it was because she had experienced and seen the life and actions of another lady's Christian faith. And here's the story.

She was a Jew running from the German Gestapo, which was invading France during World War II. She knew she was very close to being caught and had become so tired of the chase and efforts to elude her enemies that she wanted to give up. By chance she came to the home of a French Huguenot.

While there, a widow lady came to that home to say that it was time to flee to another safer hiding place. This Jewish lady said, "It's no use, they will find me anyway. They are so close behind."

The Christian widow said, "Yes, they will find someone here, but it's time for you to leave. Go with these people to safety. I will take your identification and wait here."

The Jewish lady then understood the plan . . . the Gestapo would come and instead of finding her they would find this Christian widow with her identification papers and think she was the fleeing Jew.

As Professor Riggins listened to this story, the Christian lady of Jewish descent looked him in the eye and said, "I asked her why she was doing that and the widow responded, 'It's the least I can do; Christ has already done that and more for me.'"

The widow was caught and imprisoned in the Jewish lady's place, allowing time for her to make her escape. Within six months of being placed in the concentration camp she was dead.

This Jewish lady never forgot the selfless act of friendship she was shown. Shortly after, she, too, became a follower of Jesus Christ and from that moment on lived her life in serving others in the slums and inner city of London. She met God through the greatest gift of friendship anyone can give . . . personal self-sacrifice. In reality, an authentic Christian lives her/his life in serving others.

Today's Quote: *It's the least I can do; Christ has already done that and more for me.* — The anonymous French Huguenot Widow

Today's Verse: He died for us so that, whether we are awake or asleep, we may live together with Him. Therefore encourage one another and build each other up, just as in fact you are doing (1 Thess. 5:10–11).

Day 14
How to Make a Difference

Charles Colson told the following story in a commencement speech at Reformed Theological Seminary in Jackson, Mississippi.

I love the illustration about a man named Jack Eckerd. A few years ago I was on the Bill Buckley television program, talking about "restitution" and criminal justice. A few days later I got a call from Jack Eckerd, a businessman from Florida who was the founder of the Eckerd Drug Chain, the second largest in America. He saw me on television and asked me to come to Florida. He agreed Florida had a criminal justice crisis and asked if I would I come down and do something about it.

And we did. We went around the state of Florida advocating criminal justice reforms, and everywhere we would go, Jack Eckerd would introduce me to the crowds and say, "This is Chuck Colson, my friend. I met him on the Bill Buckley television program. He's born again, I'm not. I wish I were." And then he'd sit down. We'd get on the airplane and I'd tell him about Jesus. We'd get off at the next stop, he'd repeat it, we'd do the same thing again. About a year later he called me up to tell me he believed that Jesus was God and had been raised from the dead. When he got through, I said, "You're born again!"

He said, "No, I'm not, I haven't felt anything."

I said, "Yes, you are! Pray with me right now."

The first thing he did was to go to one of his drugstores. There he saw *Playboy* and *Penthouse* magazines. He'd seen them many times before, but it had never bothered him.

He went back to his office, called in his president and said, "Take *Playboy* and *Penthouse* out of my stores."

The president said, "You can't mean that, Mr. Eckerd. We make three million dollars a year on these magazines."

Eckerd said, "Take 'em out of my stores." And in 1,700 stores across America those magazines were removed from the bookshelves because a man had given his life to Christ.*

By being his friend, Colson led this man to Christ *and* removed a terrible blight from 1,700 stores!

*Charles Colson, from his 1986 commencement address at Reformed Theological Seminary, Jackson, Mississippi, condensed.

Today's Quote: *No one ever attains very eminent success by simply doing what is required of him; it is the amount and excellence of what is over and above the required that determines the greatness of ultimate distinction.* — Charles Kendall Adams

Today's Verse: What good is it, my brothers, if a man claims to have faith but has no deeds? Can such faith save him? (James 2:14).

Day 15
The Sickness Is Swallowed

A medical missionary serving in Egypt was very distressed that the people he was serving continued to suffer and die from a very strange kind of anemia. He and his wife had grown to love these humble, trusting people, as they ministered to their physical and spiritual needs. All of his medical efforts to relieve the suffering and find a cure for the disease had made no difference. In his research, he learned that the disease came from a liver fluke (a parasitic flatworm like a blood-sucker) which was found to live in the soil in and around the people's water supply in their villages.

Having isolated the culprit, he wrote to John Hopkins Medical Research Center and made arrangements so that on his return to America research could be performed in the hopes of developing a cure. However, immigration authorities stopped him at the airport as he returned to the United States. They examined his luggage and asked for an explanation about the container of flukes. He explained the need for research, but their reply was, "No way! Under no circumstances are you going to bring diseased liver flukes into our country."

He begged, pleaded, and explained again, to no avail. He was faced with a decision — either destroy the flukes or not enter the country. He was allowed to go into the men's rest room to destroy, then flush the flukes down the drain. He took the top off of the container and prepared to destroy and then empty them down the sewer. . . .

Then he thought again of his many friends, patients, in Egypt and the intense suffering, death, and sorrow they were facing because of this rare disease. Without hesitation, he lifted the container to his lips and swallowed the diseased liver flukes. He then successfully made his way through customs.

Over the next five years he, too, struggled for life while he and researchers at Johns Hopkins searched for a cure. After much trial and error a cure was eventually found. Five years after coming back home he was able to return to his mission field with a cure for the dreaded disease among the beloved people of his mission.

The principle is quite simple: He was not alone in his struggle with this disease — he identified with and became one with his friends!

The major elements of friendship are empathy, compassion, caring, loving, and identification. A great friend will not ask anyone else to do what he's not willing to do himself.

Today's Quote: *Working together means winning together.*

Today's Verse: When he saw the crowds, he had compassion on them, because they were harassed and helpless, like sheep without a shepherd (Matt. 9:36).

A Hallmark Story

More than a few of the townspeople who paused to survey the burned-out ruins of the Hall brothers' Kansas City greeting card warehouse on January 12, 1915, must have commented on the poor luck of the young owners of the business. The fire that swept through the building the night before had destroyed thousands of cases of Valentine's Day cards that were soon to be shipped, bringing in money that 23-year-old wholesaler Joyce Hall and his brother, Rollie, were counting on to pay off creditors. Now, with their entire inventory lost in the blaze, the brothers would be unable to meet their $17,000 debt.

Coming when it did, the loss was particularly heartbreaking for Joyce Hall, who was just beginning to establish himself as a successful businessman after years of struggle and poverty. The Norfolk, Nebraska, native had been working since the age of nine, when his father, an itinerant preacher, abandoned the family, leaving Joyce and his two older brothers to provide for their semi-invalid mother. Young J. C. (as he preferred to be called) peddled perfume door-to-door and later went into business selling greeting cards. Seeking brighter opportunities, he took a supply of cards to Kansas City, where he began wholesaling them to local druggists. Soon he added a line of imported Christmas and Valentine's Day cards, and within a year he was joined by his brother Rollie. They gradually expanded their sales territory into nearby cities and states before the fire wiped them out.

"If you want to quit, that's a good time to quit. But if you are not a quitter, you begin to think fast," J. C. said later of the calamity. Rising to the challenge, the young businessman borrowed more money and purchased a local engraving firm so that he and Rollie could replenish their stock quickly and cheaply by printing their own greeting cards. Their first two original designs were ready in time for Christmas 1915. Sold in midwestern drugstores, the tiny (2-1/2" X 4") hand-painted Yuletide greetings were a success with holiday shoppers, providing a badly needed inflow of cash to the Halls' devastated firm.

At the time of J. C. Hall's death in 1982, his namesake firm (Hallmark) was turning out 8 million greeting cards a day! Among them is still the very first everyday card, carrying a friendship theme by Edgar Guest: "I'd like to be the kind of friend you've been to me."

Friendship is really about perseverance, and isn't it fitting that the "hallmark" of friendships is still around after these many years, because of commitment?

Today's Quote: *When you care enough to send the very best!* — J. C. Hall

Today's Verse: Lazy hands make a man poor, but diligent hands bring wealth (Prov. 10:4).

Fellowship

Here's an old down-to-earth poem which I've always liked. The author is unknown, which is too bad . . . but it talks about the happiness for life which all can experience when a person lives in such a way as to care for others:

FELLOWSHIP
When a feller hasn't got a cent
And is feelin' kind of blue,
And the clouds hang thick and dark
And won't let the sunshine thro',
It's a great thing, oh my brethren,
For a feller just to lay
His hand upon your shoulder in a friendly sort o' way.

It makes a man feel queerish,
It makes the teardrops start.
And you kind o' feel a flutter
In the region of your heart.
You can't look up and meet his eye,
You don't know what to say
When a hand is on your shoulder in a friendly sort o' way.

Oh this world's a curious compound
With its honey and its gall;
Its cares and bitter crosses,
But a good world after all.
And a good God must have made it,
Leastwise that is what I say,
When a hand is on your shoulder in a friendly sort o' way.

Feeling toward others in the friendly way suggested by this poem goes a long way, too, toward giving another a greater sense of worth, something that helps all of us know that life can be meaningful!

Today's Quote: *No one is useless in the world who lightens the burden of it for anyone else.* — Charles Dickens

Today's Verse: My yoke is easy and my burden is light (Matt. 11:30).

A friend is one who knows all about you and likes you just the same.

Elbert Green Hubbard (1856–1915)

Day 18
Arthur and Walter

Arthur and Walter were good friends, but it's Arthur who really missed out on a wonderful opportunity . . . a once-in-a-lifetime kind of opportunity. One day, Walter took his good friend Arthur for a ride out into the country. They drove off the main highway and down a small graveled road through groves of fruit trees to a large, uninhabited expanse of land. A few horses were grazing here and there as well as a few head of cattle. They could see the falling-down remains of a couple of old shacks. A tumbleweed blew across the road and dust swirled up behind the tires of the car.

Walter stopped the car, got out followed by Arthur, and began to describe with great enthusiasm and vividness the wonderful things he was going to build. He went on at great length and in extreme detail, painting word pictures. He was excited! He was enthused! He then turned to his good friend Arthur and invited him to buy some land surrounding his proposed project in order to get in on the ground floor.

But Arthur was thinking to himself: *Who in the world is going to drive 25 miles for this crazy project? The logistics of the venture are staggering!*

Walter went on explaining to his friend, Arthur, "I can handle the main project myself, but it will take all my money. In just a couple of years the land bordering it, where we're standing now, will be jammed with hotels and restaurants and convention halls to accommodate the people who will come to spend their entire vacation here at my park." He continued, "I want you to have the first chance at this surrounding acreage, because in the next five years it will increase in value several hundred times."

"What could I say? I knew he was wrong," Arthur tells the story later. "I knew that he had let this dream get the best of his common sense, so I mumbled something about a tight money situation, and promised that I would look into the whole thing a little later on."

"Later on will be too late," Walter cautioned Arthur as they walked back to the car. "You'd better move on it right now."

And so Art Linkletter turned down the opportunity to buy up all the land that surrounded what was to become Disneyland! His friend, Walt Disney, tried to convince him . . . but Art thought him crazy! So now, you, too, know the rest of that story of friendship! Incredible! Talk about a lost opportunity!

Today's Quote: *Life is what happens to you while you're busy planning more important things.*

Today's Verse: So, as the Holy Spirit says: "Today, if you hear his voice, do not harden your hearts" (Heb. 3:7–8).

Day 19
The Friendly Favor

A friend of mine recently took a business problem to a friend of his in a different business and asked for his help in solving the situation. Then, to further add insult or whatever, he told him that he was doing him a great favor and that later he would be more than happy to have the favor returned by helping this friend with any business problems he may encounter in the future of his business.

Strange . . . you may be thinking, just like I did, How can I be doing a friend a favor by giving him one of my problems? But the more you think about this the more logical it becomes. After all, when we think about it there are several good reasons for sharing problems:

1) IF that person is really a friend, he/she will be glad to help you with your problems. If a real friend, they will welcome the opportunity to help.

2) BY giving another friend your problems, you are forcing them to think, and most likely to think in a whole new field of discipline. To creatively think is one of the highest functions of the human being.

3) YOU asking the friend to take a break from their own work changes the factors of another conundrum.

4) YOU make that friend realize that you value his/her opinions, thoughts, and answers. You are giving value and worth to that friend.

5) BY helping you solve a problem, you may have given the opportunity to come up with some excellent, creative ideas regarding their own business or living.

There is a story about Benjamin Franklin, who had a powerful enemy in Philadelphia. For some reason this person hated Franklin and made no bones about it. In attempting to come up with a creative solution to turn this enemy into a friend, Dr. Ben hit on the idea of asking to borrow a book he knew the man had in his possession. When asked, this enemy was happy to share the book and the cold war was broken between the two. It wasn't long before they became friends. We all need to work on our friendships.

A man named Hall (that's all I know about his name) wrote: "A friend should be one in whose understanding and virtue we can equally confide, and whose opinion we can value at once for its justness and its sincerity. He who has made the acquisition of a judicious and sympathizing friend may be said to have doubled his mental resources."

Today's Quote: *A friend is someone with whom you dare to be yourself.*
— C. Raymond Beran

Today's Verse: Like a madman shooting firebrands or deadly arrows is a man who deceives his neighbor and says, "I was only joking!" (Prov. 26:18–19)

Day 20
Make New Friends

One mistake we tend to make is to believe that we should keep all our friends all of our life. It simply can't be done! In fact, it shouldn't be done! H.L. Mencken said, "One of the most mawkish of human delusions is the notion that friendship should be lifelong. The fact is that a man of resilient mind outwears his friendships. They become threadbare, and every act and attitude that they involve becomes an act of hypocrisy." Blunt, but right.

Maybe you disagree . . . if so, then, you might believe that a girl or boy must marry the first person she or he is infatuated with. Or, that we should all be still going around with the same bunch of friends that we went to school with. Mencken also said, "A prudent man, remembering that life is short, examines his friendships critically now and then. A few he retains, but the majority he tries to forget."

Now enters George Bernard Shaw on the same subject, "The only man who behaves sensibly is my tailor; he takes my measure anew each time he sees me, while all the rest go on with their old measurements and expect them to fit me."

To really live means changing, and changing means forming new friendships. Why? Because no two people mature at the same pace. Some people move ahead in maturation much quicker than others.

Therefore it may be too much of a stretch to attempt to retain a friendship when a new one will allow the growth to continue. Sometimes this discarding of old friendships is looked at with much guilt, or we may see it as a disloyal act, when in reality it may be the most natural and logical thing to do.

One observation is that when we grow older the friendships we form tend to be much stronger and longer-lasting than when we were young and changing and moving and discovering who we really are. The best friendships are made with people who tend to think along the same lines, believe in many of the same positives, and will constantly challenge us. These are friends we enjoy taking a long drive with, spending a pleasant evening in their company, taking to dinner, or just simply talking together.

There are friends who challenge me. There are some with whom I can violently disagree on several subjects, which only makes for more lively conversation. Having those old friends is really wonderful . . . but in some ways it's even better to look forward to making new friends.

Today's Quote: *It is not strange that even our loves should change with our fortunes.* — Shakespeare

Today's Verse: Wounds from a friend can be trusted, but an enemy multiplies kisses (Prov. 27:6).

Day 21
Your Own Mike

What does it mean to have a best friend? What is really the meaning and purpose of a true friend? Let me share this short story with you and let's see if we can answer those questions.

Mike and Tim had been friends for 20 years. They had reached the prime of their lives. Both were married, had children, owned their own businesses — life had been good to them. For over 20 years hardly a week went by without the two of them, and then their families, getting together. Tim had told many people just how lucky he was to have a friend like Mike. He truly loved Mike. Why? Because Mike was the most selfless person he had ever met. He had seen Mike's selfless lifestyle in action for the last 20 years.

Then one day tragedy struck Tim's life. His father died in his sleep, totally unexpectedly. Within an hour of his father's death Tim called Mike, and asked if he would come over. Mike said "I'm on my way."

Tim was on the front lawn of his parent's house continuing to greet people as they came to comfort the family. All things considered, Tim seemed to be doing very well. He had barely shed a tear. Suddenly, he noticed Mike's pickup coming up the long lane of his parent's farm. Tim's eyes began to tear, his heart began to pound. As Mike started to walk toward the house Tim left the crowd and started to walk toward him. When Tim reached Mike he was sobbing uncontrollably. They embraced and Mike said words of comfort to him. The people in the yard stood in silence as they witnessed what true friendship was all about — one being there for the other.

Why would Tim cry when Mike came up? What was going on? There is something about that bond of a friend where you can just be yourself, and all the walls of life come down. It was just two souls comforting one another. It is one of the most powerful unions in this world. Mike and Tim's relationship is very simple. They think of the other person first, they share with each other their thoughts, dreams, and fears, and they truly love each other.

They are lucky to have each other. How many of us can say we have a friend like this? Unfortunately, not very many. In the hustle and bustle of today's life we seem to have very little time for friends and relationships. Loyalty is not a priority, but it should be. Slow down, reach out, and start a friendship. Maybe you'll meet your own Mike.

Today's Quote: *A friend is never known until a man has need.* — John Heywood

Today's Verse: You, then, why do you judge your brother? Or why do you look down on your brother? For we will all stand before God's judgment seat (Rom. 14:10).

Last Words

July 4, 1776, is a day which all Americans can point to as a day of beginning for our country. It's a day to remember and still celebrate. Many are the names we have connected with this day. Let's take a look at just two of them — two who shared a unique friendship.

Are you aware that both John Quincy Adams and Thomas Jefferson died on the very same day, 50 years to the day after their Declaration of Independence had been adopted by Congress? Both Adams and Jefferson, having lived through so much together as patriots, statesmen, and debaters, died on July 4, 1826. They were friends for many years before bitter political disagreements divided them for decades.

Jefferson's death and Adams' was in itself a kind of curious coincidence. Jefferson died first, and legend has it that he asked for Adams. A few hours later, Adams' last words were, "Thomas Jefferson still lives." And in part it was true.

The part that remains has been left us in the writings of these two men. I doubt that the contemporaries of these men had bestowed greatness upon them, nor anything that they have said has taken greatness from them. But because of the momentous times in which they lived, their friendship is often left to gather dust. After all, Jefferson was our country's third president; Adams was the sixth. Both were diplomats, statesmen, and intellectuals.

History tells us that these were paradoxical men — sometimes troubled men. They both failed in their humanness, alienating each other over squabbles, but shared their remarkable gifts with a new nation. They are to be remembered for their greatness and not their weakness. It's good that we remember.

Jefferson designed his own gravemarker, which did not mention his presidency! In the twilight of his life, perhaps he realized that simpler things were most important.

One thing I would call to your mind is: No matter the disagreement, eternal things are what count. One day, on your deathbed, you might wish for laughter with an old friend.

Today's Quote: *May the God of the armies of Israel shower down the blessings of His divine providence on you, give you wisdom and fortitude, cover your head in the day of battle and danger, add success, convince our enemies of their mistaken measures, and that all their attempts to deprive these colonies of their inestimable constitutional rights and liberties are injurious and vain!* — Jonathan Trumbull, provincial governor to George Washington when he declared a "Continental Fast Day" on July 20, 1775.

Today's Verse: I have done what is righteous and just; Do not leave me to my oppressors (Ps. 119:121).

Day 23
"Nobody Loved Me Like Cliff Did"

Cliff had a heart for people. Driving down a busy street on the way to an important meeting, he'd routinely see someone down-and-out and forget all about the meeting and stop to help. He knew what loyalty was, and how to show it to a world that had forgotten what it was. Reaching out to people, he asked for nothing in return.

Robert was lonely. His wife had passed away, he was being phased out of the business he had started, and his grown children were doing what children do when they move away from home. Careers, families, and vacations were ahead of old Dad on the priority list.

Robert now found himself on the outside looking in. There just wasn't enough to fill the day.

Robert and Cliff met in the winter of their lives, although the latter was much younger than the former. Joining forces in a particular enterprise, the two became like father and son. Cliff asked advice. Robert received validation. They benefited from each other's friendship. Bonds were forged. For several years, Cliff gave Robert a reason to get up in the morning. Actually, he gave him several reasons; *Let's do this, let's do that. Tomorrow is important, can you be there?*

Sitting at his breakfast table early one spring day, Robert rose to answer the ringing phone. It was Cliff's wife. *Can you come? Cliff died this morning.*

As hundreds of mourners filed by the casket and extended their sympathies to the family, Robert stood patiently off to one side until most were gone, then he made his way to Cliff's widow. "Elaine," he began, taking her hand in his. "Nobody in my life loved me like Cliff did."

Wow . . . have you ever had a friend like that? One who would stick to you like glue? If you or I can find one person like that in a lifetime, we've been immeasurably blessed. That's what real friendship is: unyielding love. Hearts for each other.

What about you, friend? Do you know someone whose life is worth more than your own? Will someone say at your funeral, "Nobody loved me like _____ did"? What a jewel in your crown!

Today's Quote: *The fingers of God touch your life when you touch a friend.* — Mary Dawn Hughes

Today's Verse: And Jonathan made a covenant with David because he loved him as himself (1 Sam. 18:3).

A friend you have to buy won't be worth what you pay for him.

George D. Prentice (1802–1870)

More Important Than Being the Best

The woman was a famous movie star. She had come to visit her daughter at the summer gymnastics camp for girls that my husband and I run near Fresno, California. When the time came for the daily workouts, the actress watched her daughter from the sidelines. The girl was good, though not good enough to compete at a championship level. She was nervous.

When the girl finished, her mother called out, "That was awful. You looked like a sack of potatoes tumbling downhill." The girl burst into tears. My heart went out to her.

I found myself remembering the day one of my own gymnastic performances put me close to tears. I might have shed them, except for something my mother said to me then.

When my mother was carrying her first child, she was stricken with polio, and she has been confined to a wheelchair and crutches ever since. She never let that discourage her. She managed to raise five children and have a career as well.

I decided to join a gymnastics program. By 1972, I was on the U.S. Women's Gymnastic Team for the Olympic Games in Munich. I couldn't think of anything else except a gold medal.

It had become my habit, during practice and the warm-ups before a contest, to pray . . . asking God for the strength and control to get through the routine. That day in Munich, I was determined not to disgrace my country and myself. But, though I competed to the best of my ability, I didn't win a gold medal. I joined my parents in the stands, all set for a big cry. I managed a faltering, "I'm sorry. I did my best."

"You know that, and I know that," my mother said, "and I'm sure God knows that, too." She smiled and said ten words that I never forgot: "Doing your best is more important than being the best."

Suddenly I understood my mother better than ever before. She had never let her handicap prevent her from always doing her best.

Now I went over to the sobbing girl and put an arm around her. "Honey," I said, "I've been watching you improve all summer and I know you have done your best, and doing your best is more important than being the best. I'm proud of you."

She smiled at me through her tears. Maybe somewhere, someday, she'll pass those words along.*

*Cathy Rigby, *The Guideposts Treasury of Love* (New York, NY: Guideposts, 1978), page 24–25.

Today's Quote: *What does love look like? It has the hands to help others. It has the feet to hasten to the poor and needy. It has the eyes to see misery and want. It has the ears to hear the sighs and sorrows of men. That is what love looks like.* — St. Augustine

Today's Verse: No, in all these things we are more than conquerors through Him who loved us (Rom. 8:37).

Day 25
Starting All Over Again

Why is it that some people seem to radiate joy and enthusiasm in spite of adversity or trouble? How can it be that some people are excited all the time? These are some of the choice people that we all should be able to count as friends. Let's get into the story. The late Governor Charles Edison of New Jersey told this story about his father, a man of a resilient, undefeatable spirit — yes, the famous inventor, Thomas A. Edison.

On the night of December 9, 1914, the great Edison Industries of West Orange was virtually destroyed by fire. Thomas Edison lost two million dollars that night and much of his life's work went up in flames. He was insured for only $238,000, because the buildings had been made of concrete, at that time thought to be fireproof.

"My heart ached for him," Charles said. "He was 67 . . . not a young man . . . and everything was going up in flames. He spotted me. 'Charles,' he shouted, 'where's your mother?' 'I don't know, Dad,' I said. 'Find her,' he told me. 'Bring her here. She will never see anything like this again as long as she lives.' "

The next morning, walking about the charred embers of all his hopes and dreams, Thomas Edison said, "There is great value in disaster. All our mistakes are burned up. Thank God we can start anew."

And three weeks after the fire, his firm delivered the first phonograph! Now that's the story of a man who had learned how to face the adversities and disasters of this human existence. He also knew that 67 years were in the past . . . that the loss of money was nothing really, because there was that inner strength that would allow him to build again.

So what if life has collapsed around you, relationships have fallen apart, friendships are gone? There is always the possibility of starting all over again! Take heart, my friend. Today can be a new day! You can make a new start! The problems that have come into your life are an opportunity to give it another go. Build that friendship once more! There is always hope and help for you when you build on God's Word!

Today's Quote: *The grand essentials to happiness in this life are something to do, something to love, and something to hope for.* — Joseph Addison

Today's Verse: I have told you these things, so that in Me you may have peace. In this world you will have trouble. But take heart! I have overcome the world (John 16:33).

Day 26
Be Generous

Be generous! Give to those whom you love; give to those who love you; give to the fortunate; give to the unfortunate; yes . . . give especially to those to whom you don't want to give.

Your most precious, valued possessions and your greatest powers are invisible and intangible. No one can take them. You, and you alone, can give them. You will receive abundance for your giving. The more you give . . . the more you will have!

Give a smile to everyone you meet (smile with your eyes) . . . and you'll smile and receive smiles.

Give a kind word (with a kindly thought behind the word) — you will be kind and receive kind words.

Give appreciation (warmth from the heart) — you will appreciate and be appreciated.

Give honor, credit and applause (the victor's wreath) — you will be honorable and receive credit and applause.

Give time for a worthy cause (with eagerness) — you will be worthy and richly rewarded.

Give hope (the magic ingredient for success) — you will have hope and be made hopeful.

Give happiness (a most treasured state of mind) — you will be happy and be made happy.

Give encouragement (the incentive to action) — you will have courage and be encouraged.

Give cheer (the verbal sunshine) — you'll be cheerful and be cheered.

Give a pleasant response (the neutralizer of irritants) — you will be pleasant and receive pleasant responses.

Give good thoughts (nature's character builder) — you will be good and the world will have good thoughts for you.

Give prayer (the instrument of miracles) for the godless and the godly — you will be reverent and receive blessings, more than you deserve!

BE GENEROUS! GIVE!*

Even without worldly wealth or material possessions it's possible for you to be generous!

*W. Clement Stone, *A Treasury of Success Unlimited* (New York, NY: Hawthorne Books, 1966), page 9–10.

Today's Quote: *Of all knowledge the wise and good seek most to know themselves.* — Shakespeare

Today's Verse: For out of the overflow of the heart the mouth speaks. The good man brings good things out of the good stored up in him, and the evil man brings evil things out of the evil stored up in him (Matt. 12:34–35).

Day 27
A Horse Thief on Trial

A man in the Old West was being tried for stealing a horse. Just to refresh your memory, stealing a horse at that time was a very serious offense. A person could easily be shot by a posse or hanged if found guilty.

This gentleman was accused of stealing a horse from another man, but the man from whom he allegedly had stolen the horse was hated by every person in town. The horse owner had never done anything good for anybody other than himself, and he didn't have a single friend in town. However, the alleged thief was well-liked.

The case was presented to the jury. The evidence against the accused was pretty strong but not absolutely airtight. After about 30 minutes of deliberation, the jury returned to the court chambers. "Gentlemen and ladies of the jury, have you reached a verdict?"

"Yes, Your Honor, we have." There was a long dramatic pause, then the jury foreman continued, "We find the defendant not guilty if he will return the horse."

After the judge had silenced the laughter and cheering in the courtroom, he sternly addressed the jury, "I cannot accept this verdict. You will have to retire until you reach another verdict." The jury dutifully went back to their room to hammer out another verdict.

This time an hour had passed. I remind you that not a single person on the jury liked the man whose horse had allegedly been taken. They re-entered the courtroom and the place grew silent.

"Gentlemen and ladies of the jury," began the judge, "have you reached a verdict?"

The jury foreman stood up, "Yes, we have, Your Honor."

There was complete silence in the courtroom — you could have heard a pin drop. Everyone moved forward in their seats as they eagerly awaited the verdict.

"Well, what is your verdict?" asked the judge.

"The jury foreman pulled out his piece of paper, straightened it out, and read the decision rendered by these 12 jury members, "We find the defendant not guilty, and he can keep the horse!" Now the courtroom burst into wild cheering and laughing!

Is there a moral to the story? How about this? It pays to be interested in other people! If you spend your life only trying to take advantage of others, never caring for anybody else, you could end up a real loser — like the man who lost his horse!

Today's Quote: *No matter how useless a person may be, their friendship is worth more than their hatred.*

Today's Verse: Do not be deceived: God cannot be mocked. A man reaps what he sows (Gal. 6:7).

One Powerful, One Powerless

This story is taken from one of Chuck Colson's monthly newsletters to the supporters of his Prison Fellowship Ministry.

I was at the 120-year-old Indiana State Prison to speak. Only weeks earlier, Stephen Judy had been electrocuted there. An execution always creates a special tension in a prison and I could sense it that day. It was in the air, in the voices of the guards, in the faces of the men.

After my talk, the warden walked us through the maze of cell blocks to that most dreaded of places . . . an isolated wing where five men awaited their final decree and death. Nancy Honeytree, as well as several volunteers, came along. Finally, we were ushered through two massive steel gates into the secure area. The inmates were allowed out of the cells and we joined in a circle in the walkway while Nancy strummed the guitar and sang; it was a beautiful moment for those condemned men as she sang, "Amazing Grace."

Two of the men, I knew from their correspondence, were believers. One of them, James Brewer, had the most radiant expression during our visit and he sang at the top of his lungs.

As we were shaking hands and saying goodbye, I noticed that Brewer walked back into his cell with one of our volunteers. The others began filing out but this volunteer remained in Brewer's cell. I was expected in two hours in Indianapolis for a meeting with the governor, so I walked back into the cell. "We've got to go," I called out to the volunteer.

"Please, please, this is very important," the volunteer replied. "You see, I am Judge Clement. I sentenced this man to die. But, now he is born again. He is my brother and we want a minute to pray together."

Chuck Colson continued his story, telling of standing in the entrance to that solitary, dimly-lit cell, frozen in place. For, "here were two men . . . one black, one white; one powerful, one powerless; one who had sentenced the other to die, one ready to die. Yet there they stood grasping a Bible together, Brewer smiling so genuinely, the judge so filled with love for the prisoner at his side."*

Humanly speaking, this would be impossible . . . but Jesus Christ makes the difference in relationships!

*Chuck Colson Newsletter.

Today's Quote: *It's better to keep a friend from falling than to help him up after he falls.*

Today's Verse: The Lord would speak to Moses face to face, as a man speaks with his friend (Exod. 33:11).

Day 29
Not That Committed

This is a story about two New Yorkers, best friends, who decided that they had had it with city living, so they bought a ranch in Texas in order to live off the land like their ancestors.

The first thing they decided they needed was a mule to pull a plow. So they went to a neighboring rancher and asked him if he had any mules to sell. The rancher said, "No, sorry."

They were disappointed but continued talking with the rancher for a few minutes more. One of them spotted a bunch of honeydew melons stacked against the barn and asked, "What are those things?"

The rancher, seeing that they were city slickers, decided to have some fun. "Oh," he answered, "those are mule eggs. You take one of those eggs home and wait for it to hatch and you'll have your mule."

The city slickers were overjoyed, so they bought one of the melons, placed it in the back of their pickup, and drove down the bumpy road toward their own spread. Suddenly they hit an especially bad bump and the honeydew melon bounced out of the back of their pickup, hit the road, and busted open! Looking into his rearview mirror the driver saw what had happened and slammed on the brakes, turned the truck around and drove back to retrieve their mule egg.

Meanwhile a big old Texas jackrabbit came hopping by and saw the honeydew burst open in the road. He hopped over to it and standing in the middle of the mess began to eat it. At about that time the two city slicker friends came running toward the smashed melon and spied this long-eared Texas creature in the middle of it! One of the friends shouted, "Our mule egg has hatched! Let's get our mule!"

But seeing these two characters running toward it, the jackrabbit took off hopping in every direction, changing directions with the city slickers in hot pursuit. Give them credit, these two New Yorkers gave it everything they had . . . finally they could go no further.

Both of these good friends dropped wearily onto the ground gasping for air as they watched the jackrabbit hop off into the distance. Raising up on one elbow, one of the men said to the other, "Well, I guess we lost our mule."

The other friend nodded, grimly, "Yes, but you know," he said, "I'm not sure I wanted to plow that fast anyway."

Today's Quote: *It takes a long time to grow an old friend.* — John Leonard

Today's Verse: So I commend the enjoyment of life, because nothing is better for a man under the sun than to eat and drink and be glad. Then joy will accompany him in his work all the days of the life God has given him under the sun (Eccles. 8:15).

Day 30
One Success Formula

There is one absolute principle if you really want your life to count, if you want to live with enthusiasm, if you want to make friends. *FIND A NEED AND FILL IT! Only* six words but what a powerful concept! I would venture to say that every enterprise that has been successful has been built on this formula. Every true friendship is based on this foundation. Find people's needs and fill them! Love people! Love this wonderful world! Love God.

To see how this works in real life, let's stop at Ed's Place . . . nothing but a little diner in a big city — greasy spoon, plain and simple, stools at a counter. Let's sit down.

Consider Ed . . . resting his big hands on the counter he asks, "Okay, brother (sister), what'll you have?"

"Are you Ed?"

"Yep."

"They tell me you have good hamburgers here."

"Brother, you never ate such a burger."

"Okay, let me have one, everything on it."

Then we notice, also at the counter sits an old man who looks miserable. He is hunched over, hands shaking. After Ed puts the burger in front of us, he places his hand in a friendly way on the old man's shoulder. "That's all right, Bill," we hear him say, "everything is all right. I'll get you a bowl of nice hot soup right away."

Another old man shuffles up to pay. Ed says, "Now Mr. Land, watch the cars out there. They're pretty fast at night." Then he adds, "Have a look at the moonlight on the river. It's pretty tonight."

When we pay our check . . . one of us remarks, "I like the way you talked to those old men. You made them feel that life is good."

"Why not?" Ed asks. "Life is good. Me, I get a kick out of living. Our place is sort of like home to them. Anyway, I kind of like 'em."

Believe in yourself, believe in life, believe in people, believe in God. Practice the principle of our concept! Practice these principles and discover that real enthusiasm becomes a part of your life! Believe that your life can be improved, believe that your job can be improved, believe that you can become a better person, believe that you can help others by finding their needs and helping to fill them! What a way to live! Go for it!

Today's Quote: *The power of positive thinking is stronger in fighting disease than all of the technology of modern medicine.* — Thomas W. Allen

Today's Verse: A cheerful heart is good medicine, but a crushed spirit dries up the bones (Prov. 17:22).